LIVING IN THE WILD: SEA MAMMALS

DOLPHINS

Anna Claybourne

Raintree is an imprint of Capstone Global Library Limited, a company incorporated in England and Wales having its registered office at 7 Pilgrim Street, London, EC4V 6LB – Registered company number: 6695582

www.raintreepublishers.co.uk
myorders@raintreepublishers.co.uk

Text © Capstone Global Library Limited 2013
First published in hardback in 2013
First published in paperback in 2014
The moral rights of the proprietor have been asserted.

Edited by Adam Miller, Andrew Farrow, and Laura Knowles
Designed by Steve Mead
Picture research by Mica Brančić
Original illustrations © Capstone Global Library Ltd 2013
Illustrations by HL Studios
Originated by Capstone Global Library Ltd
Printed and bound in China by CTPS

ISBN 978 1 406 25008 4 (hardback)
16 15 14 13 12
10 9 8 7 6 5 4 3 2 1

ISBN 978 1 406 25015 2 (paperback)
17 16 15 14
10 9 8 7 6 5 4 3 2 1

British Library Cataloguing in Publication Data
Claybourne, Anna.
Dolphins. -- (Living in the wild. Sea Mammals)
599.5'3-dc23
A full catalogue record for this book is available from the British Library.

Acknowledgements
We would like to thank the following for permission to reproduce photographs: Alamy pp. 16 (© Steve Taylor ARPS), 18 (© Karen van der Zijden), 32 (© Jan Carroll);Ardea pp. 23 (© Augusto Leandro Stanzani), 25 (© Augusto Stanzani); Getty Images pp. 6 (Photographer's Choice/Mike Hill), 11 (Oxford Scientific/ Gerard Soury), 13 (Peter Arnold/Mark Carwardine), 12 (Barcroft USA/Kevin Schafer), 14 (Photolibrary/Cliff Philipiah), 27 (Time & Life Pictures/Alan Levenson), 35 (Ed Kashi), 38 (WaterFrame/ Reinhard Dirscherl), 40 (age fotostock/Juan Carlos Munoz), 41 (The Image Bank/Stephen Frink); Nature Picture Library pp. 15 (© Andy Rouse), 20 (© Doug Perrine), 21 (© Doug Perrine), 22 (© Doug Perrine), 24 (© Doug Perrine), 26 (© Doug Perrine), 28 (© Brandon Cole), 29 (© Brandon Cole), 30 (© Doug Perrine), 34 (© Hugh Pearson), 37 (© Todd Pusser), 39 (© Jeff Rotman), 42 (© Chris Gomersall), 45 (© Mark Carwardine); Photoshot p. 9 (Oceans Image/Mauricio Handler); Shutterstock p. 4 (© A Cotton Photo).

Cover photograph of a bottlenose dolphin sticking its head above water reproduced with permission of Getty Images/ Grambo Grambo.

Data reproduced in the map on p. 31 supplied courtesy of R.W. Baird/www.cascadiaresearch.org.

Every effort has been made to contact copyright holders of any material reproduced in this book. Any omissions will be rectified in subsequent printings if notice is given to the publisher.

Contents

Some words are shown in bold, **like this**. You can find out what they mean by looking in the glossary.

What are sea mammals?

Sea mammals are a group of animals that mainly live in seas and oceans. They include seals and sea lions, walruses, sea otters, polar bears, whales, and dolphins. They are all brilliant at swimming and holding their breath to dive under water. They are sometimes called marine mammals, as "marine" means to do with the sea.

This **pod** of spotted dolphins are playing together underwater, but need to swim up to the surface of the sea to breathe.

Being a mammal

Mammals are a type of animal. Humans are mammals, and so are dogs, cats, and mice. All mammals breathe air. They are usually furry or hairy, and mother mammals make milk in their bodies to feed their babies. Mammals are also warm-blooded, meaning they can keep their bodies warmer than their surroundings.

Sea mammals do all these things too, but often in different ways. For example, whales and dolphins have hardly any hair, with just a few small hairs around their faces. Having less hair helps them to swim faster. And instead of breathing through their mouths, they have **blowholes** on the tops of their heads.

LIFE IN THE SEA

Around half of all the living things on Earth are found in the sea, and scientists often discover new sea creatures.

Meet the sea mammals

There are around 130 different types, or **species**, of sea mammal. They have **adapted** in different ways to live in the sea:

Type of sea mammal	How do they move?	Where do they live?
Whales and dolphins	use tail, fins, and flippers	These sea mammals live in water all the time.
Manatees and dugongs	use tail and flippers	
Seals, sea lions, and walruses	use flippers	These sea mammals spend some of their time in water, and some on land.
Sea otters	use legs and tail	
Polar bears	use legs	

What are dolphins?

Dolphins are sea mammals that spend all their lives in the water. Dolphins look like fish, because they have adapted so well to life in the water. Their smooth, fish-shaped bodies help them zoom quickly through the sea. They flap their powerful tails up and down to push themselves forward, and use their flippers to steer. Many dolphins can even leap right up into the air before splashing back down.

SPOT THE DIFFERENCE

It is easy to confuse dolphins with large fish, such as sharks, but there are some key differences:
- Dolphins' tail flukes are horizontal. Sharks and other fish have upright tail flukes.
- Unlike most fish, dolphins have rounded heads and beak-like snouts.
- Dolphins have blowholes on their heads, and fish do not.

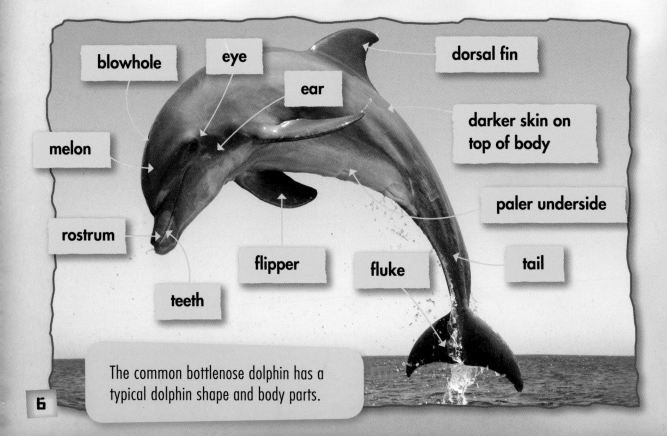

blowhole eye ear dorsal fin

melon darker skin on top of body

rostrum paler underside

teeth flipper fluke tail

The common bottlenose dolphin has a typical dolphin shape and body parts.

The dolphin's family

Dolphins and whales belong to a group of sea mammals called **cetaceans**. They have existed for about 50 million years. They developed when some types of early land mammal, similar to a hippo, switched to living in the water.

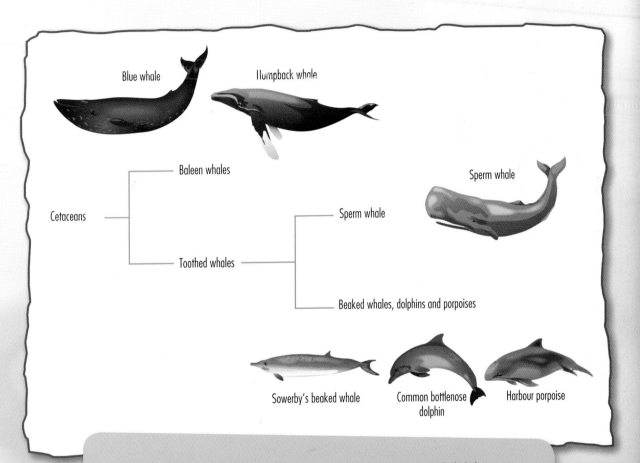

Blue whale

Humpback whale

Sperm whale

Cetaceans

Baleen whales

Toothed whales

Sperm whale

Beaked whales, dolphins and porpoises

Sowerby's beaked whale

Common bottlenose dolphin

Harbour porpoise

There are about 130 species of cetaceans, or whales and dolphins. They are divided into two main groups. Dolphins belong to the "toothed whale" group. Baleen whales, such as the humpback whale, have no teeth. Porpoises are similar to dolphins, but usually smaller.

How are dolphins classified?

Scientists sort out, or **classify**, all living things into different groups, to show how they are related. The groups get smaller and smaller until they pinpoint one particular species.

You can show how a type of living thing is classified using a triangle diagram, like this. At the top is the largest group dolphins belong to, the animal kingdom. As you go down, the classification narrows into smaller groups, such as mammals, cetaceans, and dolphins.

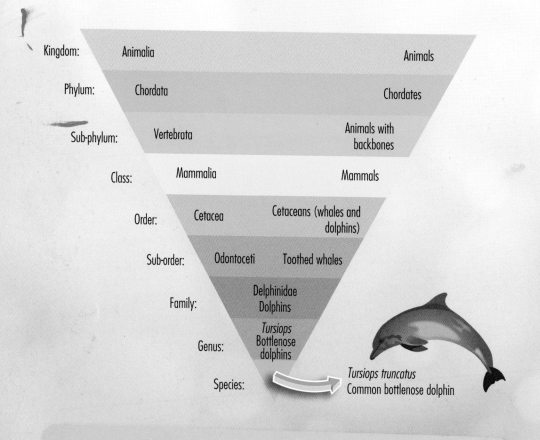

Kingdom:	Animalia	Animals
Phylum:	Chordata	Chordates
Sub-phylum:	Vertebrata	Animals with backbones
Class:	Mammalia	Mammals
Order:	Cetacea	Cetaceans (whales and dolphins)
Sub-order:	Odontoceti	Toothed whales
Family:	Delphinidae	Dolphins
Genus:	*Tursiops*	Bottlenose dolphins
Species:		*Tursiops truncatus* Common bottlenose dolphin

This diagram shows all the groups that the common bottlenose dolphin belongs to, from the biggest down to the smallest.

How many dolphins?

There are nearly 40 different species, or types, of dolphin altogether. Some of them are known as whales, but actually belong to the dolphin family. The killer whale or orca, for example, is a type of large dolphin. The family also includes some unusual-looking dolphins, such as the spotted dolphin, and the pink-coloured "boto", or Amazon River dolphin.

The spotted dolphin is found all over the world. Its Latin name is *Stenella attenuata*. Only the adults have spots, not the babies.

Where do dolphins live?

Dolphins are very common, and live in seas and oceans all around the world. Most species avoid the very coldest seas near the North and South Poles, but a few types, such as orcas, do live there.

Shallow or deep?

Some dolphins, such as Hector's dolphin, prefer to stay in shallower water closer to the shore. Others, such as spinner dolphins, can be found far out in the middle of the ocean. Dolphins cannot breathe under water, so they must come to the surface regularly for air. They don't dive down to the deepest depths of the ocean. They usually stay in the "sunlit zone", the upper 200 metres (650 feet) of the sea. This is also where it is easiest to find fish, a dolphin's favourite food.

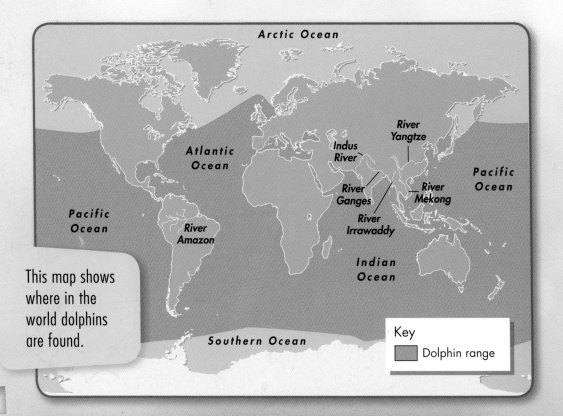

This map shows where in the world dolphins are found.

Arctic Ocean

Atlantic Ocean

Pacific Ocean

Pacific Ocean

River Amazon

Indus River

River Ganges

River Irrawaddy

River Yangtze

River Mekong

Pacific Ocean

Indian Ocean

Southern Ocean

Key

Dolphin range

Home habitats

Some species of dolphin like to stick to a particular area, or **habitat** (type of surroundings). For example, the unusual-looking Irrawaddy dolphin likes to live around **estuaries** and river mouths in Southeast Asia, and is rarely seen anywhere else. A few dolphin species even live in large rivers, such as the Amazon.

Irrawaddy dolphins are quite small, but have very large, rounded heads. They have dark eyes and tiny dorsal fins.

DOLPHIN-SPOTTING

People can often spot dolphins in seaside bays, inlets and estuaries, and narrow channels between islands. Look out for their rounded triangle-shaped **dorsal fins** sticking out of the water. If you're on a boat, watch for dolphins swimming alongside or behind it. They do this to ride on the boat's bow waves, or to feed on fish the boat stirs up in the water.

River dolphins

Most dolphins live in salty seawater, but a few live in rivers. Some of these "river" dolphins are also found in salty estuaries, or in both rivers and seas. They developed from sea dolphins, but gradually moved up into rivers and adapted to live in fresh (non-salty) water.

The river dolphins include:
- the Amazon River dolphin, found in the Amazon **basin** in South America
- the South Asian river dolphin, found in the Indus and Ganges rivers in Asia
- the Baiji, found in China's Yangtze River, which is probably now **extinct**
- the Franciscana or La Plata dolphin. This dolphin belongs to the river dolphin family, but actually lives in salty estuaries and around coasts in South America.

The Amazon River dolphin is the biggest river dolphin, growing up to 2.5 metres (8 feet) long. Some of this species are bright pink, making them look amazing.

Different dolphins

You can tell river dolphins belong to the dolphin family, but they do have some differences. They are usually smaller, as they have adapted to living in smaller spaces. They have long, narrow snouts and very small eyes, as they rely on their other senses to find **prey** in the murky river water. In fact, the South Asian river dolphin is almost blind.

GOODBYE BAIJI

The Baiji or Yangtze River dolphin is, or was, the rarest river dolphin. It is sadly now probably extinct, or almost extinct. Fishing activities and **pollution** in the busy river are thought to have wiped it out. No Baijis have been spotted since 2002.

The pale-coloured Baiji was about the size of a human, with a very rounded forehead and long snout.

What adaptations help dolphins survive?

Adaptation means changing. Species of living things change gradually over time. Some become better suited to their surroundings, while others die or move elsewhere. This is why so many animals fit their habitats so well. Dolphins are a great example.

Life in the water

Dolphins have developed a long, **streamlined** body shape that slips through water easily. Their skin is smooth, not furry, as this would slow them down. Instead of fur, they have a thick layer of fat called **blubber** under their skin to keep them warm.

Living in salty seawater means dolphins can take in too much salt as they feed. To get rid of it, the salt comes out in their **urine** (wee). In fact, dolphin urine is saltier than seawater.

Dolphins can blow out air and breathe in again very quickly when they surface. The breath they breathe out of their blowholes is called "blow".

Breathing

Dolphins cannot breathe through their mouths. They can only breathe through their blowholes, which are actually adapted nostrils. Over millions of years, their nostrils moved to the tops of their heads, making it easier to swim and breathe at the same time.

When a dolphin dives into cold water, a process called the **mammalian diving reflex** begins. The dolphin's heart slows and reduces the flow of blood around its body, using up less **oxygen**. This helps dolphins to hold their breath for up to 10 minutes at a time.

DIVE LIKE A DOLPHIN

Other mammals have a mammalian diving reflex too, including humans. When we dive into cold water, our heart rate slows down and we can hold our breath for longer – though not as long as a dolphin.

Dolphins have incredibly strong tails. By swishing its tail, a dolphin can zoom through the water, make amazing leaps, or even "tail-walk" like this.

Fighting and biting

Dolphins have many small, cone-shaped teeth – up to 250 of them, depending on the species. They are perfect for gripping onto slippery prey such as fish and squid. Dolphins also sometimes use their teeth for fighting each other.

Sea sounds

Most dolphins can see well, but their hearing is even better. They detect prey and other objects by making clicking noises, then sensing the echoes when the sounds hit something and bounce back. This method, called **echolocation**, is very useful in the sea as sound travels fast through water, and the sea can be murky and dark.

HOW OLD AM I?

Every year, a dolphin's teeth grow a new layer, a bit like the rings inside a tree trunk. Scientists can tell how old a dolphin is from the layers in its teeth.

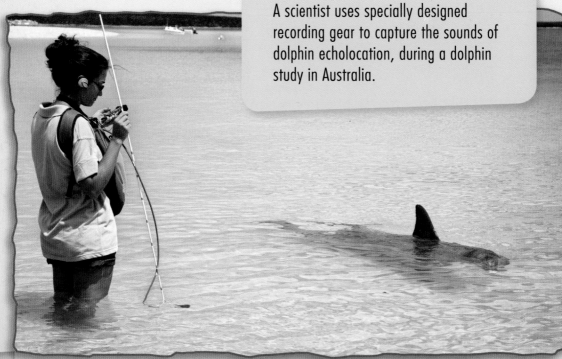

A scientist uses specially designed recording gear to capture the sounds of dolphin echolocation, during a dolphin study in Australia.

Dolphins get their familiar rounded head shape from a large, fatty organ in their forehead, called the **melon**. It is made of a fatty, yellow substance. Scientists think it works a bit like a lens, focusing the clicking sounds into narrow beams, and sending them out into the water in different directions.

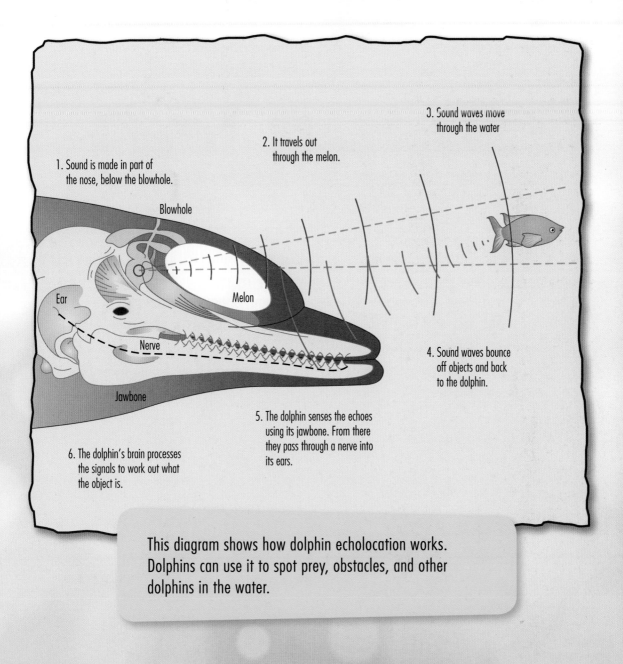

3. Sound waves move through the water

2. It travels out through the melon.

1. Sound is made in part of the nose, below the blowhole.

Blowhole

Melon

Ear

Nerve

Jawbone

4. Sound waves bounce off objects and back to the dolphin.

5. The dolphin senses the echoes using its jawbone. From there they pass through a nerve into its ears.

6. The dolphin's brain processes the signals to work out what the object is.

This diagram shows how dolphin echolocation works. Dolphins can use it to spot prey, obstacles, and other dolphins in the water.

What do dolphins eat?

Dolphins are **carnivores** – hunters that catch and eat other animals. They mainly feed on small fish, but will also snap up squid, prawns, crabs, or octopuses. Orcas, the biggest type of dolphin, will hunt and eat seals, turtles, and even other dolphins and whales.

Dolphins use their teeth to catch and grab onto their food, but they don't chew it. They swallow each mouthful whole, usually gulping down each fish in one go. Dolphins prefer to eat fish headfirst, probably so that the tail, spines, and fins go down easily and don't hurt their throats.

How much?

Dolphins eat around 5 per cent of their body weight each day, but a hungry mother who is feeding her baby on milk may eat more – up to 8 per cent of her body weight. This means that a large male bottlenose weighing 500 kilograms (1,100 pounds), needs about 25 kilograms (55 pounds) of fish a day – or around 150 sardines.

This bottlenose dolphin is flipping a huge, delicious salmon into the right position, before gobbling it up.

Sometimes humans catch so many fish that dolphins run out of food. Fishermen have even killed dolphins because they hunt the same fish species that humans want to catch.

FOOD CHAINS AND WEBS

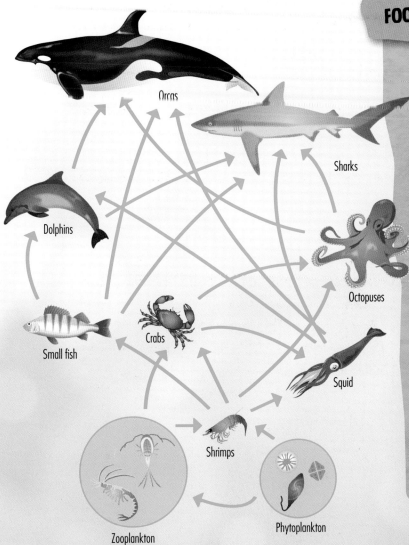

Orcas

Sharks

Dolphins

Octopuses

Small fish

Crabs

Squid

Shrimps

Zooplankton

Phytoplankton

In the sea, as in other habitats, living things depend on each other for food. Dolphins eat smaller sea creatures, such as mackerel and other fish. These fish eat even smaller fish or shrimps, which themselves eat **zooplankton** and **phytoplankton** that float in the sea. A sequence like this is called a **food chain**. Together, a habitat and the group of living things it supports are called an **ecosystem**. In most ecosystems, many food chains combine to form much bigger **food webs**.

Going hunting

To find food, dolphins roam around in the sea, sometimes swimming long distances. They follow shoals of fish or look for cold water **currents** where lots of fish are found.

As they get closer, dolphins use eyesight or echolocation (see page 17) to home in on their prey. They may also try to stun larger fish by thrashing at them with their tails. Once the prey is within reach, a dolphin will quickly seize and snap it up.

Dolphins round up and dive through a huge shoal of fish, trying to snap up their dinner.

Small fish that swim in large shoals are often called schooling fish, forage fish, or baitfish.

Working together

Dolphins often travel in groups and hunt as a team. They surround a shoal of fish then take turns to dart through the shoal to feed. Sometimes they herd the fish into shallow water and trap them there.

In a few parts of the world, dolphins even cooperate with humans who are fishing in shallow water. The dolphins gather where the fish are, showing the fishermen where to cast their nets. The fishermen then share their catch so that the dolphins get a reward.

Fat fish

Dolphins' favourite food is fatty fish such as mackerel. They contain the most energy, so dolphins don't need to catch and eat as much. Less fatty options, such as squid and octopus, contain less energy so dolphins have to catch more of them.

FOOD CLUES

Dolphins feed under water, so it is hard for scientists to discover which fish species they are eating. Sometimes they look inside dead dolphins' stomachs to see what they last fed on. Scientists can also take samples of dolphin blubber and study it to find clues about the dolphin's diet.

What is a dolphin's life cycle?

Dolphins don't lay eggs. Like humans and most other mammals, they give birth to live young called calves. To have a calf, a male and a female dolphin have to get together and mate.

Dolphins mate at any time of year, but especially in spring and autumn. Groups of dolphins gather together, and males and females begin to call, chase, scratch, and nudge each other, before forming pairs. However, they don't just stick to one mate. Each male dolphin may mate with several females.

This male and female spinner dolphin pair play together before mating.

Birth of a baby

After being pregnant for almost a year, a mother dolphin gives birth. Most dolphins have just one calf at a time. The calf comes out of its mother tail-first, so that it doesn't have to hold its breath for long while it is being born. As soon as it is out, the mother lifts her baby to the surface to breathe.

The father dolphin doesn't stay with the mother or help look after the calf. Instead, the female usually joins a group, or pod, of other dolphins. They surround and support her to keep her and her baby safe. Sometimes another dolphin, known as an "auntie" (although it can occasionally be male), will help the mother to give birth and care for her calf.

In this amazing photo you can see a baby bottlenose dolphin halfway through being born. Its tail and dorsal fin have already emerged, and the rest of its body will be out in a few seconds.

23

Milk from mum

Mother dolphins feed their babies on milk, as all mammals do. But how can the calf drink the milk under water? The milk comes from teats on the mother's underside. To feed, the calf wraps its tongue around the teat so that it is firmly attached, and the milk squirts into its mouth. The milk is very creamy and full of fat, so the calf grows fast. A baby dolphin doubles in weight between birth and two months old.

A spotted dolphin mother swims along with her calf, protecting it from danger. When it is older, the calf will develop spots like its parents.

Swimming together

Dolphin calves are in danger of being eaten by **predators** such as sharks, so they swim close to their mothers to stay safe. When feeding, they swim underneath her body. Otherwise, they swim just above and to one side of her. In this position, the "echelon position", the mother's movement helps to pull the calf along, so it uses up less energy.

Mothers and calves stay close together and often stroke, snuggle, and cuddle up to each other.

Mothers with young calves often form a group called a nursery pod. They care for, guard, and even feed each other's babies. Younger adults can also act as babysitters. Scientists think this helps them learn for when they become parents themselves.

Learning

Baby dolphins cannot do everything straight away. They must learn to balance in the water, breathe quickly using their blowholes, and use echolocation. Each calf also develops its own special whistling call, which other dolphins can recognize.

LIFE STAGES

- Calves feed on milk for three or four years.
- They begin feeding on fish, as well as milk, at around four months old.
- By 10 to 12 years of age, most dolphins are adults and ready to mate.
- Dolphins can live for up to 50 years.

How do dolphins behave?

Dolphins are famous for their fascinating behaviour. They live in groups, make friends, and "speak" to each other. They are clever, good at learning, and like playing, too. This could explain why so many people love dolphins – they remind us of ourselves.

This pod of striped dolphins are leaping and splashing together as they travel in the Atlantic Ocean.

Dolphin pods

Dolphins are **social** animals. They get together in pods, or groups, to travel, hunt, play, mate, and look after their calves. A pod can range from just a handful of dolphins up to 30 or more, and dolphins often leave one pod and join another. Sometimes, many pods join together to form huge herds of hundreds of dolphins. Dolphins can be very attached to others in their pod, and sometimes seem to make "best friends" with another dolphin.

Helping each other

The dolphins in a pod look out for each other. If one is hurt or sick, the others will surround and support it, and hold it up to the sea surface when it needs to breathe.

Dolphins can make all kinds of whistling, clicking, creaking, squeaking, and "quacking" sounds using their noses and blowholes. Some are used for echolocation (see page 16–17), but most are for communicating. Dolphins appear to have conversations, making a series of different noises and replying to each other. Scientists are busy trying to discover what they are saying!

LOUIS HERMAN

Dolphin expert Louis Herman has studied dolphins for decades, especially bottlenose dolphins, which are known for their intelligence. He has made many discoveries about dolphin senses, behaviour, and "language", such as what kinds of meanings dolphins can understand.

Louis Herman at work in Hawaii, interacting with two dolphins.

Having fun

Dolphins are incredibly playful, and seem to spend a lot of their time having fun. They chase and nudge each other, and "surf" on waves or on the swell created by ships. They throw coral, fish, or ocean litter to each other to catch. They also love leaping out of the water and splashing back in.

Playing can be useful to help animals learn things, especially clever animals such as dolphins. A game of catch, for example, could help them practise echolocation and grabbing objects, making them better at hunting. Playing with other dolphins is also a way to be friendly and close to each other. This is important for dolphins. They need to rely on, and not fall out with, the others in their pod. However, dolphins may also simply play for fun, and to avoid getting bored.

This small group of spotted dolphins are nuzzling and swimming around each other. Scientists think dolphins may do this to show caring and friendliness to each other.

Half asleep

Dolphins have a strange, but sensible, way of sleeping. A sleeping dolphin wouldn't be able to come to the surface to breathe and could be snapped up by a shark. So instead, dolphins sleep with one half of their brain at a time. They close one eye, and give the opposite side of their brain a rest. The other side stays awake and the other eye stays open.

Dolphins may leap and jump around just for fun, as humans sometimes do.

A DAY IN THE LIFE OF A BOTTLENOSE DOLPHIN

Common bottlenose dolphins are among the best known of all dolphin species. They can be found all around the world and are what many people imagine when they think of a dolphin. What dolphins do, and when, depends on the season, the tides, and whether they are male, female, older, younger, or looking after a calf. However, an average day for a bottlenose usually follows a pattern.

When a dolphin opens its mouth wide like this, you know it's not happy. It's a threat display to warn other dolphins off.

EARLY MORNING TO MIDDAY

Dolphins have a breakfast-time hunting and feeding session. They will dive under water to catch fish for between a few seconds and a few minutes at a time, depending on whether they are in deep or shallow water.

In the middle of the day, dolphins roam around, explore, and play with the other dolphins in their pod. If they are looking for a mate, male dolphins might fight each other instead of playing. This is mixed with short periods of rest or sleep, sometimes in pairs.

LATE AFTERNOON AND NIGHT

Dolphins often start hunting and feeding again in the late afternoon. They may also go hunting at night, as some fish come closer to the surface then. They spend some time asleep, too.

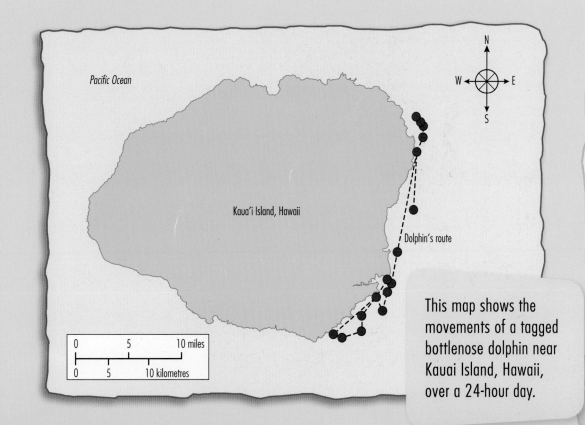

Pacific Ocean

Kaua'i Island, Hawaii

Dolphin's route

0   5   10 miles

0   5   10 kilometres

This map shows the movements of a tagged bottlenose dolphin near Kauai Island, Hawaii, over a 24-hour day.

How intelligent are dolphins?

It is difficult to measure intelligence in animals. Scientists argue about how smart dolphins really are, but they do seem to be very intelligent, and can certainly do some amazing things.

Big brains don't always equal intelligence, but clever animals often have big brains compared to their body size. They also have a large cortex – the part of the brain used for thinking. Dolphins score highly on both these measures. In fact, their brain-to-body-weight percentage is ahead of some other animals we consider clever, such as chimpanzees and elephants.

Captive dolphins in aquariums, like this bottlenose, can learn tricks such as standing up on their tails to "shake hands" with a trainer.

Learning and changing

The more intelligent an animal is, the less it relies on **instinct** (behaviour it is born with) and the more it learns. Dolphins are very good at learning. Calves learn many skills from adults, like human babies. Dolphins can also invent new hunting methods and teach them to each other, and learn to perform tricks. Like humans, intelligent animals such as dolphins are also more helpless when they are young. They need their parents to care for them, feed them, and help them learn.

Brilliant bottlenose

Bottlenose dolphins are among the most intelligent dolphin species. Some bottlenose live in aquariums and learn to do amazing tricks, such as leaping out of the water in pairs, or balancing on their tails. Although this shows off their skill, living in **captivity** is thought to be stressful for them.

MILITARY DOLPHINS

Some bottlenose dolphins have been trained to work for the US Navy, locating underwater mines and collecting equipment from the seabed. Their brilliant diving and echolocation skills make them better at doing this than humans. They are rarely harmed, but some people think it is wrong to use dolphins in this way.

Dolphin language

Scientists have used lots of interesting experiments to try to work out what dolphin sounds mean. They also try to "talk" to dolphins themselves to see how much they can understand. In one test, dolphin expert Louis Herman and his team taught bottlenose dolphins a kind of sign language, using hand signals. They could then "speak" to the dolphins in short sentences and give them instructions, which they understood.

Using tools

Not many animals use tools, and it is seen as a sign of high intelligence. Bottlenose dolphins in Shark Bay, Australia have shown they can do it. They started holding sea sponges over their snouts and then snuffled through the mud for food. The sponges protect their noses from sharp rocks. Scientists have found that one female dolphin invented the method, then taught it to others.

A Shark Bay dolphin shows off its natural sponge nose-protector, used to help it find prey on the seabed among the sharp rocks.

Clever Kelly

A dolphin named Kelly amazed scientists in a research centre with her cleverness. The dolphins were trained to bring litter in their tank to the surface, in exchange for a fish reward (to stop them from swallowing the litter, which could be dangerous). But Kelly began storing litter under a rock instead. She then tore off small pieces and swapped them for fish, getting herself lots of rewards instead of one!

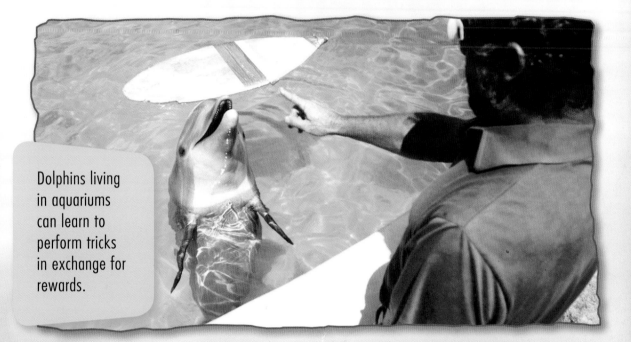

Dolphins living in aquariums can learn to perform tricks in exchange for rewards.

SPEAK DOLPHIN

Experts think dolphins sometimes use sounds in these ways:

Type of call	Meaning
Creaking noise	I'm over here! (to help mothers find their calves)
Squeak-squeak-squeak	I'm feeling stressed or alarmed
Bzzz-bzzz-bzzz	Don't mess with me!
Yelp-yelp-yelp	I'm looking for a mate
Whistle	It's me! (each dolphin has its own "signature" whistle)

What threats do dolphins face?

Being a dolphin can be pretty dangerous. Besides their natural enemies, they face many new threats. Most are caused by human activities, which are thought to kill many thousands of dolphins every year.

Human activity

People are increasingly hunting dolphins to eat, especially when fish supplies run low. Dolphins are sometimes hunted to use as bait, or to protect fish supplies. People still also catch dolphins to sell to aquariums. The ones they don't sell often end up being killed for meat.

ENDANGERED DOLPHINS

Not all dolphins are **endangered**, but some species are at risk of dying out, and some are even becoming extinct. Dolphins at risk include the Irrawaddy, humpbacked, and Hector's dolphins, and the South Asian river dolphin.

The fishing industry can affect dolphins. If a fishing net drags a dolphin under water, it will drown. Thousands of dolphins die each year in nets designed for tuna or other fish. When overfishing takes place and humans catch so many fish that they begin to disappear, dolphins can run out of food.

Pollution problem

Dolphins can die from choking on or swallowing ocean litter. Waste chemicals from factories and farms flowing into seas or rivers can also make them ill. Sound pollution is also a problem, with noises from ships, oil drilling, and seabed mining confusing dolphins and damaging their hearing.

Getting lost

Boats taking tourists to spot dolphins sometimes disturb them and force them away from their natural habitats. Many dolphins also die from getting stuck on beaches, though scientists are not sure why this happens.

To survive and be healthy, dolphins need clean, peaceful seas, with a good food supply and plenty of space to roam around in.

How can people help dolphins?

People have done a lot of harm to dolphins. But we can help them by changing the way we treat them, and the ways we use the sea. One way to help wildlife is to create a wildlife reserve or national park. This often happens on land, but parts of rivers, coasts, and oceans can also be protected. In a protected marine area, hunting is banned. Activities like fishing, sailing, and seabed exploration are sometimes allowed, but only if they are done carefully and don't affect protected species.

This pod of bottlenose dolphins is swimming safely in the blue waters of a marine reserve in the Red Sea.

Changing the law

It takes a long time to change laws, but gradually, many countries are making it illegal to hunt dolphins. They can also use laws to reduce the amount, and type, of pollution released into the sea. If a chemical is found to be especially harmful, it can be banned altogether.

How can you help dolphins?

- Adopt a dolphin! Adopters pay to help run a dolphin study centre, sanctuary, or other area where dolphins live.
- Choose dolphin-friendly products. Look for labels that show fish such as tuna has been caught without harming dolphins.
- Reduce, reuse, and recycle to reduce pollution and **global warming**.
- Never drop litter off boats — it could harm dolphins. Of course, you shouldn't drop litter at all!
- Support wildlife charities that campaign to protect endangered species.

LEARNING MORE

It is important for scientists to study dolphins so that we know which species are in trouble and what they need to survive. Some research centres that study dolphins let volunteers help with their work. If you really love dolphins, maybe you could even become a dolphin scientist yourself.

This marine scientist is taking a blood sample from a bottlenose dolphin to learn more about dolphin health.

What does the future hold for dolphins?

In the modern world, many wild animals are at risk of dying out and becoming extinct. Some dolphin species are among them, while others, like the bottlenose, are still quite common. But this could change if the threats to dolphins get worse.

Sadly, it is probably too late to save the Baiji, a river dolphin from China. Other species, such as Hector's dolphin, could die out too, unless we work hard to protect them. Even common species could become extinct if too many of them are hunted or caught in nets.

However, people around the world are doing a lot to protect dolphins. Hunting them is mostly banned, and there are increasing numbers of safe reserves.

The Commerson's dolphin, with its striking black and white markings, is one of the species that has suffered from hunting and being caught in fishing nets.

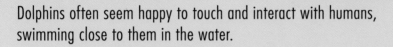

Cap

Dolphins often seem happy to touch and interact with humans, swimming close to them in the water.

Global warming

Besides the other problems they face, dolphins could be badly affected by global warming. This is the Earth's rising temperature. In the ocean, cooler water holds more oxygen, and more fish can live in it. So, as the seas get warmer, there may be fewer fish, and less food for dolphins. But no one yet knows exactly how this will turn out, or how bad it will be.

LOVEABLE DOLPHINS

In one way, dolphins are lucky. They are popular, much-loved animals. People like and admire them, and are keen to help them. Some other animals need just as much help, but people are not as attracted to them.

Adaptable dolphins

On the plus side, dolphins are smart and adaptable. They can learn, change their behaviour, and invent solutions to problems. So maybe as the world changes, some dolphin species will learn to live in new ways to help them survive.

curved dorsal fin

distinctive "criss-cross" pattern makes a V-shape under the dorsal fin

black and grey upper body

short, wide tail

melon

short, tapered beak

blowhole

powerful body

groove or dent between melon and beak

black teardrop markings around eyes

cream and white underside

Short-beaked common dolphin

The short-beaked common dolphin is a typical marine or sea dolphin. It is a widespread species, living in most parts of the world, and it is often seen leaping and splashing at the sea surface. It is a fast swimmer, with a strong, streamlined body, a small pointed snout, and beautiful black, grey, cream and white skin markings.

Species: short-beaked common dolphin

Latin name: *Delphinus delphis*

Nicknames: crisscross dolphin, saddleback dolphin

Length: 1.7 to 2.2 metres (5.5 to 7.2 feet)

Weight: around 100 kilograms (220 pounds)

Habitat: coastal and deep water in warm and **temperate** seas, with a temperature of 10 degrees Celsius or more at the surface

Diet: small fish, squid, and octopuses

Range: most of the world's seas and oceans, apart from the Indian Ocean

Life expectancy: 35 to 40 years

Amazon River dolphin

The bold, playful Amazon River dolphin, also known as the boto, is highly adapted to river life. It has excellent echolocation for finding fish in muddy water, and sensitive snout hairs that help it detect prey. It is not very speedy, but its body is super-flexible, making it good at swimming among river rocks and roots, and wriggling out of danger.

Species: Amazon River dolphin

Latin name: *Inia geoffrensis*

Nickname: boto, bufeo, pink river dolphin

Length: 1.8 to 2.5 metres (5.9 to 8.2 feet)

Weight: 100 to 200 kilograms (220 to 440 pounds)

Habitat: slow-moving tropical rivers and streams

Range: the Amazon and Orinoco river basins in South America

Diet: river fish, turtles, and crabs

Interesting fact: the Amazon river dolphin has a flexible neck. It is the only type of dolphin able to turn its head almost 180 degrees.

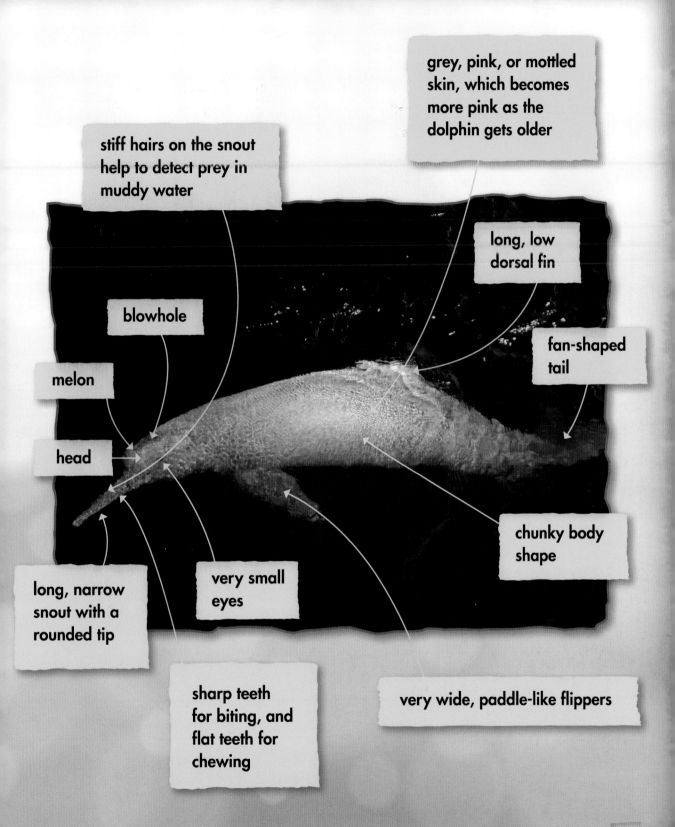

grey, pink, or mottled skin, which becomes more pink as the dolphin gets older

stiff hairs on the snout help to detect prey in muddy water

long, low dorsal fin

blowhole

fan-shaped tail

melon

head

chunky body shape

long, narrow snout with a rounded tip

very small eyes

sharp teeth for biting, and flat teeth for chewing

very wide, paddle-like flippers

Glossary

adapt change to suit the surroundings and situation

basin a river, the rivers that flow into it, and all the land around them

blowhole breathing hole in the top of a whale or dolphin's head

blubber layer of fat under the skin that helps to keep an animal warm

captivity somewhere animals are kept, such as a zoo or aquarium

carnivore animal that eats other animals

cetacean whale or dolphin

classify sort into groups

current flow of water within the sea

dorsal fin fin on a dolphin's back, also found on sharks and other fish

echolocation sense that uses sound echoes to detect objects

ecosystem habitat and the group of things that live together in it

endangered at risk of dying out

estuary large sea inlet, leading to a river

extinct no longer existing

flukes two flat, blade-like parts of a dolphin's (or whale's) tail

food chain sequence in which one creature eats another, which eats another, and so on

food web network of intertwined food chains

global warming rising temperature of the Earth

habitat type of place or surroundings that a living thing prefers to live in

instinct type of behaviour that is automatic and built in, not learned

life expectancy average length of life

mammalian diving reflex body response that helps mammals save oxygen when they swim under water

melon fatty organ in a dolphin's forehead, used in echolocation

organism living thing

oxygen gas found in air and water, which animals need to breathe in

phytoplankton tiny plant-like organisms that live in seawater

pod group of dolphins

pollution harmful waste that can end up in the sea

predator living thing that hunts and eats other living things

prey living things that are eaten by other living things

rostrum dolphin's beak or snout

social friendly and happier living in groups

species particular type of living thing

streamlined smooth and tapered, like a fish

temperate of medium warmth; not very hot or very cold

urine wee

zooplankton tiny animal-like organisms that live in seawater

Find out more

Books

A Pod of Dolphins (Animals in Groups), Richard Spilsbury (Raintree, 2012)

Endangered! Dolphins, Johannah Haney (Marshall Cavendish, 2010)

Whales, Dolphins, and Porpoises, Mark Carwardine (Dorling Kindersley, 2010)

Websites

animal.discovery.com/features/dolphins/dolphins.html
Explore the interactive dolphin information on this website, with multimedia such as dolphin sounds.

kids.nationalgeographic.com/kids/stories/animalsnature/dolphin-language/
The National Geographic Kids' website has a fascinating story about dolphin communication, with links to videos and games.

www.bbc.co.uk/nature/life/Common_Bottlenose_Dolphin
Watch video clips of bottlenose dolphins in action on the BBC website.

www.imms.org/forstudent.php
The Institute for Marine Mammal Studies' website has dolphin FAQs, tips on becoming a marine mammal scientist, and some fun games and activities.

Organizations to contact

Sea Watch Foundation: Adopt a Dolphin
www.adoptadolphin.org.uk/
The Sea Watch Foundation provides a chance to adopt a dolphin in the UK, along with competitions, fundraising tips, and how to visit real-life dolphins.

WDCS International
www.wdcs.org
The Whale and Dolphin Conservation Society has lots of campaigns, competitions, a kidzone, and an adopt-a-dolphin scheme.

Index